BANANA
— RECIPES —

**Enjoy more than 60 delicious recipes made
with this good-for-you tropical fruit**

Publications International, Ltd.

Pictured on the front cover *(clockwise from top left):* Banana Chocolate Chip Buttermilk Pancakes *(page 5)*, Bananas Foster Freeze *(page 95)*, Banana Split Ice Cream Sandwiches *(page 89)* and Chocolate and Banana Cream Layered Pie *(page 83)*.

Pictured on the back cover *(top to bottom):* Fruit Salad with Creamy Banana Dressing *(page 81)*, Strawberry-Banana Granité *(page 99)* and Cinnamon-Sugar Triangles with Caramelized Bananas *(page 117)*.

ISBN-13: 978-1-68022-692-8

Library of Congress Control Number: 2016946231

Manufactured in China.

8 7 6 5 4 3 2 1

Microwave Cooking: Microwave ovens vary in wattage. Use the cooking times as guidelines and check for doneness before adding more time.

Preparation/Cooking Times: Preparation times are based on the approximate amount of time required to assemble the recipe before cooking, baking, chilling or serving. These times include preparation steps such as measuring, chopping and mixing. The fact that some preparations and cooking can be done simultaneously is taken into account. Preparation of optional ingredients and serving suggestions is not included.

CONTENTS

BREAKFAST AND BRUNCH

BANANA CHOCOLATE CHIP BUTTERMILK PANCAKES

Makes 24 pancakes (about 6 to 8 servings)

2½ cups all-purpose flour

⅓ cup sugar

1½ teaspoons baking powder

1 teaspoon baking soda

½ teaspoon ground cinnamon

1½ cups buttermilk

3 eggs

1 teaspoon vanilla

1½ cups mashed bananas (about 3 medium)

Vegetable oil

¾ cup milk chocolate chips, plus additional for garnish

Butter and/or maple syrup

1. Combine flour, sugar, baking powder, baking soda and cinnamon in large bowl. Whisk buttermilk, eggs and vanilla in medium bowl. Gradually whisk buttermilk mixture into flour mixture until smooth. Fold in bananas.

2. Heat oil on griddle or in large skillet over medium heat. Pour ¼ cupfuls of batter 2 inches apart onto griddle. Place about 10 chocolate chips on each pancake. Cook 2 to 3 minutes or until lightly browned and edges begin to bubble. Turn over; cook 2 minutes or until lightly browned. Repeat with remaining batter and chocolate chips. Serve with butter and/or maple syrup. Top with additional chocolate chips.

Breakfast Pom Smoothie

BREAKFAST POM SMOOTHIE

Makes 1 (1½-cup) serving

1 small ripe banana	**¾ cup pomegranate juice**
½ cup frozen mixed berries	**⅓ to ½ cup soymilk or milk**

Combine banana and berries in blender; process until smooth. Add juice and soymilk; process until smooth. Serve immediately.

HARVEST FRUIT BARS

Makes 32 bars

1 package (6 ounces) diced dried mixed fruit bits	**1½ cups QUAKER® Oats (quick or old fashioned, uncooked)**
1 cup chopped banana (about 2 medium)	**1 cup (2 sticks) butter, softened**
⅔ cup TROPICANA® or DOLE® Orange Juice*	**1 cup packed brown sugar**
1½ teaspoons apple pie spice or ground cinnamon, divided	**½ cup chopped nuts** **If using old fashioned oats, decrease orange juice to ½ cup.*
1¾ cups all-purpose flour	

1. HEAT oven to 375°F. Combine dried fruit, banana, orange juice and 1 teaspoon apple pie spice in medium bowl. Set aside.

2. COMBINE flour, oats and remaining ½ teaspoon apple pie spice in medium bowl; mix well. Beat margarine and brown sugar in large bowl with electric mixer until creamy. Add oat mixture; beat until crumbly. Reserve ¾ cup mixture for topping. Press remaining oat mixture onto bottom of ungreased 13×9-inch baking pan. Bake 13 to 15 minutes or until light golden brown.

3. SPREAD fruit mixture evenly over crust to within ¼ inch of edge. Add nuts to reserved topping mixture; mix well. Sprinkle over fruit; pat down lightly.

4. BAKE 16 to 20 minutes or until golden brown. Cool completely; cut into bars.

BANANA BREAD
⌇ OATMEAL ⌇

Makes 6 servings

3 cups fat-free (skim) milk

3 tablespoons firmly packed
   brown sugar

¾ teaspoon ground cinnamon

¼ teaspoon ground nutmeg

¼ teaspoon salt (optional)

2 cups QUAKER® Oats
   (quick or old fashioned,
   uncooked)

1 cup mashed ripe bananas
   (about 3 medium)

2 tablespoons coarsely
   chopped toasted pecans

**Nonfat plain or vanilla
yogurt (optional)**

Banana slices (optional)

Pecan halves (optional)

1. Bring milk, brown sugar, cinnamon, nutmeg and salt, if desired, to a gentle boil in medium saucepan (watch carefully); stir in oats. Return to a boil; reduce heat to medium. Cook 1 minute for quick oats, 5 minutes for old fashioned oats, or until most liquid is absorbed, stirring occasionally.

2. Remove oatmeal from heat. Stir in mashed bananas and chopped pecans. Spoon into six cereal bowls. Top with yogurt, sliced bananas and pecan halves, if desired.

COOK'S TIP: To toast nuts, spread in single layer on cookie sheet. Bake at 350°F about 6 to 8 minutes or until lightly browned and fragrant, stirring occasionally. Cool before using. Or, spread in single layer on microwave-safe plate. Microwave on HIGH (100% power) 1 minute; stir. Continue to microwave on HIGH, checking every 30 seconds, until nuts are fragrant and brown. Cool before using.

SUNRISE PIZZA

Makes 4 servings

2 **DOLE® Bananas, peeled**	2 **teaspoons honey**
4 **frozen whole wheat waffles**	**Dash ground cinnamon**
¼ **cup whipped cream cheese**	**DOLE® Fresh or Frozen**
1 **can (11 oz.) DOLE®**	**Raspberries or**
Mandarin Oranges,	**Blueberries (optional)**
drained	

1. SLICE bananas on diagonal.

2. PREPARE waffles according to package directions.

3. SPREAD waffles with cream cheese. Arrange banana slices on top, overlapping.

4. ARRANGE orange segments in center of each pizza. Drizzle with honey. Sprinkle with cinnamon. Garnish with raspberries or blueberries, if desired.

STRAWBERRY-BANANA
～ PANCAKES ～

Prep Time: 10 minutes • Start to Finish: 20 minutes

Makes 16 pancakes

½ cup POLANER® All Fruit
   Strawberry Spreadable
   Fruit

½ banana, sliced

1 cup water

½ teaspoon cinnamon

2 cups pancake mix

Mix spreadable fruit, banana, water and cinnamon in a large bowl.

Preheat griddle or skillet on medium heat. Spray with cooking spray.

Add pancake mix to wet mixture. Stir until just mixed. For each pancake, spoon about ¼ cup pancake batter onto griddle. Cook until golden brown, about 2 to 3 minutes per side.

TIPS: Top with additional spreadable fruit and banana slices for a great start to your day. Add additional water to the mixture for thinner pancakes.

WHOLE GRAIN BANANA
⸺ FRUIT 'N' NUT BARS ⸺

Makes 24 bars

- 1¼ **cups whole wheat flour**
- 2 **teaspoons pumpkin pie spice**
- ½ **teaspoon baking soda**
- ¼ **teaspoon salt**
- ½ **cup (1 stick) light butter**
- ⅔ **cup firmly packed brown sugar**
- 1 **large egg**

- 1¼ **cups mashed ripe bananas (about 3 small bananas)**
- 1½ **cups QUAKER® Oats (quick or old fashioned, uncooked)**
- ⅔ **cup chopped pitted dates or golden raisins**
- ⅔ **cup chopped toasted walnuts**

1. Heat oven to 350°F. Lightly spray 13×9×2-inch metal baking pan with nonstick cooking spray. Stir together flour, pumpkin pie spice, baking soda and salt in medium bowl; mix well. Set aside.

2. Beat butter and brown sugar in large bowl with electric mixer until well blended. Add egg and bananas; mix well. (Mixture will look curdled.) Add flour mixture; beat on low just until well blended. Stir in oats, dates and walnuts. Spread evenly in prepared pan.

3. Bake 20 to 25 minutes, until edges are golden brown and wooden pick inserted in center comes out with a few moist crumbs clinging to it. Cool completely in pan on wire rack. Cut into bars.

NOTE: To store, wrap tightly in foil and store up to 2 days at room temperature. For longer storage, label and freeze in airtight container up to 3 months. Defrost, uncovered, at room temperature.

COOK'S TIP: To toast nuts, spread in single layer on cookie sheet. Bake at 350°F about 6 to 8 minutes or until lightly browned and fragrant, stirring occasionally. Cool before using. Or, spread in single layer on microwave-safe plate. Microwave on HIGH (100% power) 1 minute; stir. Continue to microwave on HIGH, checking every 30 seconds, until nuts are fragrant and brown. Cool before using.

PEANUT BUTTER AND JELLY
FRENCH TOAST

Prep Time: 25 minutes • Cook Time: 10 minutes

Makes 6 servings

1 banana, sliced

2 tablespoons peanuts, chopped

2 tablespoons orange juice

1 tablespoon honey

6 slices whole wheat bread

¼ cup grape jelly (or favorite flavor)

¼ cup peanut butter

2 eggs

¼ cup milk

2 tablespoons butter

1. Combine banana, peanuts, orange juice and honey in small bowl; set aside. Spread three slices of bread with jelly and three slices with peanut butter. Press peanut butter and jelly slices together to form three sandwiches; cut each sandwich in half diagonally.

2. Beat eggs and milk in shallow bowl. Dip sandwiches in egg mixture. Melt butter on large nonstick griddle or skillet over medium-high heat. Cook 2 minutes on each side or until lightly browned.

3. Top with banana mixture just before serving.

⚜ BANANA SPLIT ⚜
BREAKFAST BOWL

Makes 4 servings

2½ **tablespoons sliced almonds**

2½ **tablespoons chopped walnuts**

3 **cups vanilla yogurt**

1⅓ **cups sliced strawberries (about 12 medium)**

2 **bananas, sliced**

½ **cup drained pineapple tidbits**

1. Spread almonds and walnuts in single layer in small heavy skillet. Cook and stir over medium heat 2 minutes or until lightly browned. Immediately remove from skillet; cool completely.

2. Spoon yogurt into serving bowl. Layer with strawberries, bananas and pineapple. Sprinkle with toasted almonds and walnuts.

NOTE: There's no need to put aside your favorite recipes until berry season comes around; recipes like this one can be made with fresh or frozen strawberries. Frozen fruits are economical, convenient and available year-round—they are harvested at their peak of ripeness and can be stored in the freezer for 8 to 12 months.

BANANA WALNUT
⌁ MUFFINS ⌁

Makes 12 muffins

½ **cup (1 stick) unsalted butter, softened**

1 **cup packed light brown sugar**

2 **eggs, at room temperature**

1 **teaspoon vanilla**

3 **ripe bananas**

¼ **cup sour cream**

2 **cups all-purpose flour**

2 **teaspoons baking powder**

½ **teaspoon baking soda**

½ **teaspoon ground cinnamon**

¼ **teaspoon ground nutmeg**

¼ **teaspoon salt**

1 **cup coarsely chopped toasted walnuts***

*To toast walnuts, spread in single layer in heavy-bottomed skillet. Cook and stir over medium heat 1 to 2 minutes or until nuts are lightly browned. Remove from skillet immediately. Cool before using.

1. Preheat oven to 375°F. Line 12 standard (2½-inch) muffin pan cups with paper baking cups.

2. Beat butter in large bowl until soft and fluffy. Add brown sugar; beat until light and fluffy. Lightly beat eggs and vanilla in small bowl. Add to butter mixture in two batches, blending well after each addition and scraping down sides of bowl.

3. Mash bananas in separate medium bowl. Add sour cream; mix until smooth. Add banana mixture to butter mixture; beat until smooth, scraping down sides of bowl. Combine flour, baking powder, baking soda, cinnamon, nutmeg and salt in large bowl. Add flour mixture to butter mixture in three batches, blending well after each addition. Stir in walnuts. Divide evenly among prepared muffin cups, filling to top.

4. Bake 25 to 30 minutes or until toothpick inserted into centers comes out clean. Cool 10 minutes in pan on wire rack; remove to wire rack to cool completely. Store in airtight container between sheets of waxed paper at room temperature for up to 4 days. Freeze for longer storage.

TROPICAL PARFAIT

Prep Time: 10 minutes

Makes 4 servings

1½ cups orange or vanilla nonfat yogurt

1 can (11 ounces) mandarin orange segments in light syrup, drained and chopped

1 can (8 ounces) pineapple chunks in juice, drained

1 medium banana, sliced

2 tablespoons shredded coconut, toasted

1. Combine yogurt and oranges in medium bowl.

2. Spoon half of yogurt mixture into four serving bowls; top with pineapple. Spoon remaining yogurt mixture over pineapple; top with banana slices. Sprinkle with coconut. Serve immediately.

TIP: To toast cononut, spread in single layer in heavy-bottomed skillet. Cook and stir over medium heat 1 to 2 minutes until lightly browned. Remove from skillet immediately. Cool before using.

FRENCH TOAST MUFFINS WITH BANANAS AND PEANUT BUTTER SYRUP

Makes 4 servings

½ **cup milk**

2 **eggs**

1 **teaspoon vanilla**

¼ **teaspoon ground nutmeg**

4 **multigrain or whole wheat English muffins, split**

1 **teaspoon unsalted butter**

1 **large (9-inch) banana, peeled and thinly sliced**

¼ **cup chunky or creamy peanut butter**

¼ **cup maple syrup**

1. Preheat oven to 200°F. Whisk milk, eggs, vanilla and nutmeg in shallow dish or pie plate until well blended. Place 2 split muffins in dish; turn to coat. Let stand 2 minutes.

2. Melt butter in large nonstick skillet over medium heat. Remove muffins from egg mixture, allowing excess to drip off; add to skillet. Place remaining 2 split muffins in egg mixture; turn to coat. Let stand while cooking first batch 2 minutes per side or until golden brown. Remove to two serving plates; place in oven to keep warm. Repeat with remaining muffins.

3. Top French toast with banana slices. Place peanut butter in small microwavable bowl; microwave on HIGH 15 to 20 seconds until warm. Gradually stir in syrup until smooth. Drizzle over bananas and French toast.

Berry-Banana Breakfast Smoothie

BERRY-BANANA BREAKFAST SMOOTHIE

Makes 2 servings

1 container (6 ounces) berry-flavored yogurt

1 ripe banana, sliced

½ cup milk

Place yogurt, banana and milk in blender; blend until smooth. Pour evenly into two glasses. Serve immediately.

PB BANANA MUFFINS

Makes 18 muffins

¾ cup all-purpose flour

¾ cup whole wheat flour

1 teaspoon baking soda

½ teaspoon salt

¾ cup reduced-fat creamy peanut butter

2 ripe bananas, mashed (about 1 cup)

½ cup packed brown sugar

½ cup plain nonfat yogurt

1 egg

¼ cup honey

¼ cup vegetable oil

1 teaspoon vanilla

1. Preheat oven to 375°F. Line 18 standard (2½-inch) muffin cups with paper baking cups or spray with nonstick cooking spray.

2. Combine all-purpose flour, whole wheat flour, baking soda and salt in medium bowl; mix well. Beat peanut butter, bananas, brown sugar, yogurt, egg, honey, oil and vanilla in large bowl with electric mixer at medium speed until smooth and well blended. Add flour mixture; beat on low speed just until combined. Spoon batter evenly into prepared muffin cups.

3. Bake 15 to 18 minutes or until toothpick inserted into centers comes out clean. Cool in pans 5 minutes. Remove to wire racks; cool completely.

'NANA CAKES

CHOCOLATE-BANANA-PEANUT BUTTER POKE CAKE

Makes 12 to 15 servings

1 package (about 15 ounces) chocolate cake mix, plus ingredients to prepare mix

½ cup (1 stick) butter, softened

½ cup peanut butter (not natural)

4 to 5 teaspoons vanilla

1 to 2 cups powdered sugar

1 package (4-serving size) banana cream instant pudding and pie filling mix, plus ingredients to prepare mix

1. Prepare and bake cake mix according to package directions for 13×9-inch pan. Cool completely.

2. Meanwhile, beat butter in medium bowl with electric mixer at medium speed until light and fluffy. Add peanut butter and vanilla; beat 2 minutes or until fluffy. Gradually beat in powdered sugar, ¼ cup at a time, until frosting is spreadable consistency. Set frosting aside.

3. Poke holes in cake at ½-inch intervals with wooden skewer. Prepare pudding mix according to package directions. Pour pudding over cake. Top cake with peanut butter frosting. Refrigerate 2 to 3 hours or until firm.

BANANA CAKE

2½ **cups all-purpose flour**

1 **tablespoon baking soda**

½ **teaspoon salt**

1 **cup granulated sugar**

¾ **cup packed brown sugar**

½ **cup (1 stick) butter, softened**

2 **eggs**

1 **teaspoon vanilla**

3 **ripe bananas, mashed (about 1⅔ cups)**

⅔ **cup buttermilk**

1 **container (16 ounces) dark chocolate frosting**

1. Preheat oven to 350°F. Spray two 8-inch round cake pans with nonstick cooking spray.

2. Combine flour, baking soda and salt in medium bowl. Beat granulated sugar, brown sugar and butter in large bowl with electric mixer at medium speed until well blended. Add eggs and vanilla; beat until blended. Stir in bananas. Alternately add flour mixture and buttermilk; beat until well blended after each addition. Pour batter into prepared pans.

3. Bake 35 minutes or until toothpick inserted into centers comes out clean. Cool in pans 10 minutes; remove to wire racks to cool completely.

4. Fill and frost cake with chocolate frosting.

FRESH BANANA CAKE WITH SEAFOAM FROSTING

Makes 6 servings

CAKE

- 1 package (18.5 ounces) yellow cake mix
- ⅛ teaspoon baking soda
- 2 eggs
- ¾ cup COCA-COLA®
- 1 cup (2 to 3) mashed ripe bananas
- 2 teaspoons lemon juice
- ⅓ cup finely chopped nuts

SEA FOAM FROSTING

- 2 egg whites
- 1½ cups firmly packed light brown sugar
- ⅛ teaspoon cream of tartar
- ⅓ cup COCA-COLA®
- Dash salt
- 1 teaspoon vanilla extract

For cake, combine cake mix, baking soda and eggs in large mixing bowl.

Stir *Coca-Cola*® until foaming stops; add to batter. Blend ingredients just until moistened; beat at high speed of electric mixer for 3 minutes, scraping bowl often.

Combine mashed bananas with lemon juice. Add to cake batter with nuts; beat 1 minute at medium speed. Turn batter into a generously greased and lightly floured 13×9×2-inch pan.

Bake at 350°F about 40 minutes or until cake tests done. Cool on rack 15 minutes, remove cake from pan and turn right side up on rack to finish cooling.

For frosting, combine all ingredients except vanilla in top of double boiler; beat 1 minute at high speed with electric mixer. Place over boiling water (water should not touch bottom of top part); beat on high speed about 7 minutes or until frosting forms peaks when beater is raised.

Remove from boiling water (for smoothest frosting, empty into large bowl). Add vanilla and continue beating on high speed until thick enough to spread, about 2 minutes. Spread on sides and top of cooled banana cake.

BANANA CREAM
CAKE ROLL

Makes 12 servings

CAKE

1 tablespoon powdered sugar

1 cup all-purpose flour

1 teaspoon baking powder

¼ teaspoon salt

3 eggs

1 cup granulated sugar

⅓ cup water

1 teaspoon vanilla

FILLING

1 cup milk

1 package (4-serving size) vanilla instant pudding and pie filling mix

1 cup thawed frozen whipped topping

2 small bananas, thinly sliced

Chocolate curls (optional)

CAKE

1. Preheat oven to 375°F. Grease and flour 15×10×1-inch jelly-roll pan; set aside. Sprinkle powdered sugar over clean tea towel to cover at least 15×10 inches; set aside.

2. Combine flour, baking powder and salt in medium bowl; set aside. Beat eggs in medium bowl with electric mixer at medium speed 5 minutes or until thick and lemon colored. Gradually beat in granulated sugar. Beat in water and vanilla. Beat in flour mixture just until smooth. Spread in prepared pan.

3. Bake 11 to 13 minutes or until cake springs back when lightly touched. *Do not overbake.* Immediately loosen cake from edges of pan with knife; turn upside down onto prepared towel. While hot, carefully roll cake and towel from lengthwise end. Cool on wire rack at least 30 minutes.

FILLING

4. Whisk milk and pudding mix in medium bowl about 30 seconds or until thickened. Fold in whipped topping.

5. Unroll cake. Spread filling over cake to within 1 inch of edges. Arrange banana slices evenly over filling. Roll up cake using towel to guide cake. Remove cake to large sheet of plastic wrap; wrap in plastic wrap. Cover; refrigerate at least 1 hour but no more than 4 hours. Slice cake into 12 pieces. Garnish with chocolate curls.

CARROT BANANA
⌇ DUMP CAKE ⌇

Makes 12 servings

1 **package (about 15 ounces) carrot cake mix, plus ingredients to prepare mix**

1 **teaspoon baking soda**

2 **bananas, mashed (about 1 heaping cup)**

1 **cup chopped walnuts**

½ **cup raisins**

Prepared cream cheese frosting, warmed (optional)

Additional chopped walnuts (optional)

1. Preheat oven to 350°F. Grease and flour 12-cup (10-inch) bundt pan.

2. Prepare cake mix according to package directions. Stir baking soda into mashed bananas; add to batter and beat until well blended. Stir in 1 cup walnuts and raisins. Pour batter into prepared pan.

3. Bake 40 to 45 minutes or until toothpick inserted near center comes out clean. Cool in pan 10 minutes; invert onto wire rack to cool completely. Drizzle frosting over cake; sprinkle with additional walnuts, if desired.

CHOCOLATEY BANANAS FOSTER CAKE

Makes 12 servings

1 package (about 18 ounces) devil's food cake mix

1 cup mashed bananas*

3 eggs

⅓ cup vegetable oil

¼ cup water

¼ cup packed brown sugar

2 tablespoons butter

¾ cup finely chopped firm ripe bananas

½ teaspoon rum extract

¼ teaspoon ground cinnamon

2 cups whipping cream

¼ cup powdered sugar

*Overripe bananas provide the most intense banana flavor.

1. Preheat oven to 350°F. Coat two 8-inch round cake pans with nonstick cooking spray.

2. Beat cake mix, mashed bananas, eggs, oil and water in large bowl with electric mixer at low speed 30 seconds. Beat at medium speed 2 minutes. Pour batter into prepared pans. Bake 23 to 25 minutes or until toothpick inserted into centers comes out clean. Cool in pans 15 minutes. Remove to wire racks; cool completely.

3. Combine brown sugar and butter in small saucepan over medium-low heat; cook and stir until smooth. Add chopped bananas, rum extract and cinnamon; cook and stir until mixture thickens slightly. Cool completely.

4. Beat cream and powdered sugar in medium bowl with electric mixer at high speed until stiff peaks form.

5. Place one cake layer on serving plate. Spread with half of whipped cream; spoon banana mixture evenly over cream. Top with remaining cake layer. Frost cake with remaining whipped cream. Store leftovers in refrigerator.

ENLIGHTENED BANANA
⟿ UPSIDE-DOWN CAKE ⟾

Makes 12 servings

1¼ cups sugar, divided

1 tablespoon water

2 tablespoons butter

2 small bananas, cut into ¼-inch slices

1½ cups all-purpose flour

2 teaspoons baking powder

½ teaspoon salt

¼ cup canola oil

¼ cup unsweetened applesauce

2 egg whites

1 egg

½ cup buttermilk

1 teaspoon vanilla

1. Preheat oven to 325°F.

2. Combine ½ cup sugar and water in small saucepan. Heat over medium-high heat, stirring mixture and swirling pan, until mixture is amber in color. Stir in butter. Immediately pour into 8-inch square nonstick baking pan. Arrange banana slices in sugar mixture.

3. Sift flour, baking powder and salt into medium bowl. Beat remaining ¾ cup sugar, oil and applesauce in large bowl with electric mixer at medium speed 1 minute. Beat in egg whites and egg, one at a time, until blended. Beat in buttermilk and vanilla. Gradually add flour mixture; beat 1 minute or until blended. Pour batter over bananas in pan.

4. Bake 30 to 35 minutes or until toothpick inserted into center comes out clean. Cool 5 minutes in pan on wire rack; invert onto serving plate. Cool slightly; cut into 12 pieces. Serve warm or at room temperature.

CHOCOLATE ANGEL
FRUIT TORTE

Makes 12 servings

1 **package (16 ounces) angel food cake mix**

½ **cup unsweetened cocoa**

2 **bananas, thinly sliced**

1½ **teaspoons lemon juice**

1 **can (12 ounces) evaporated milk, divided**

⅓ **cup sugar**

¼ **cup cornstarch**

1 **egg**

3 **tablespoons sour cream**

3 **teaspoons vanilla**

3 **large kiwis, peeled and thinly sliced**

1 **can (11 ounces) mandarin orange segments, rinsed and drained**

1. Prepare cake according to package directions, mixing cocoa with dry ingredients. Cool completely. Cut horizontally in half to form two layers; set aside.

2. Place banana slices in medium bowl. Add lemon juice; toss to coat. Set aside.

3. Combine ¼ cup evaporated milk, sugar and cornstarch in small saucepan; whisk until smooth. Whisk in remaining evaporated milk. Bring to a boil over high heat, stirring constantly. Boil 1 minute or until mixture thickens, stirring constantly. Reduce heat to medium-low.

4. Blend ⅓ cup hot milk mixture and eggs in small bowl. Add to saucepan. Cook 2 minutes, stirring constantly. Remove saucepan from heat. Let stand 10 minutes, stirring frequently. Add sour cream and vanilla; blend well.

5. Place bottom half of cake on serving plate. Spread with half of milk mixture. Arrange half of banana slices, kiwi slices and mandarin orange segments on milk mixture. Place remaining half of cake, cut side down, over fruit. Top with remaining milk mixture and fruit.

BANANA PECAN BUNDT
WITH BUTTER SAUCE

Makes 16 servings

CAKE

- **1 cup chopped pecans, toasted***
- **1 package (about 18 ounces) yellow cake mix without pudding in the mix**
- **1⅓ cups water**
- **5 eggs**
- **¾ cup mashed ripe bananas (2 medium bananas)****
- **½ cup puréed sweet potatoes**
- **2 tablespoons vegetable oil**

BUTTER SAUCE

- **¼ cup apple cider, apple juice or bourbon**
- **¾ cup sugar**
- **½ cup (1 stick) butter**
- **¼ cup milk**

*To toast pecans, spread in single layer on baking sheet. Bake in preheated 350°F oven 8 to 10 minutes or until golden brown, stirring frequently. Cool before using.

**Do not use overripe bananas.

1. Preheat oven to 325°F. Generously coat 10-inch bundt pan with nonstick cooking spray. Sprinkle nuts evenly in bottom of pan.

2. Combine cake mix, water, eggs, bananas, sweet potatoes and oil in large bowl; beat according to package directions. Pour batter evenly into prepared pan.

3. Bake 55 to 60 minutes or until toothpick inserted into center comes out clean. Cool 15 minutes in pan on wire rack. Gently loosen sides and center of cake with knife; invert onto wire rack to cool completely.

4. Combine apple cider, sugar, butter and milk in small saucepan over medium-high heat. Cook and stir until butter is melted and sugar is dissolved. Serve warm sauce over cake slices.

TIP: The sauce may be made in advance and refrigerated. To serve, reheat over medium heat.

CARIBBEAN CAKE SQUARES

Makes 16 servings

1 package (9 ounces) yellow cake mix

½ cup orange juice

2 egg whites

2 cans (8 ounces each) crushed pineapple in juice

1 tablespoon cornstarch

½ cup slivered almonds

½ cup flaked coconut

2 large ripe bananas

1 can (15 ounces) mandarin orange segments in light syrup, drained

1. Preheat oven to 350°F. Spray 13×9-inch baking pan with nonstick cooking spray.

2. Beat cake mix, orange juice and egg whites in medium bowl with electric mixer at medium speed until smooth and well blended. Pour into prepared pan.

3. Bake 11 to 12 minutes or until toothpick inserted into center comes out clean. Cool completely in pan on wire rack.

4. Drain juice from pineapple into 2-cup measure; reserve crushed pineapple. Stir juice into cornstarch in small saucepan until smooth. Bring to a boil over high heat, stirring constantly. Boil 1 minute, stirring constantly. Remove from heat.

5. Toast almonds and coconut in small skillet over medium heat 3 to 4 minutes or until golden brown, stirring frequently.

6. Spread pineapple evenly over cake. Slice bananas and arrange over pineapple. Top with mandarin oranges. Carefully drizzle pineapple juice mixture evenly over top. Sprinkle with almonds and coconut.

7. Cover and refrigerate at least 1 hour before serving. Cut into 16 pieces.

BANANA NUT CAKE WITH BROWN SUGAR TOPPING

Makes 12 to 15 servings

CAKE

- 3 cups all-purpose flour
- 1½ cups packed brown sugar, divided
- 3 bananas, mashed
- 1 cup chopped nuts
- ½ cup white chocolate chips
- ½ cup oil
- ¼ cup milk
- 1 egg
- 1 teaspoon baking soda

TOPPING

- 1⅔ cups packed brown sugar
- ½ cup butter
- ½ cup chopped nuts

1. Preheat oven to 350°F. Grease and flour 10-inch round baking pan.

2. For cake, beat flour, 1½ cups brown sugar, bananas, 1 cup chopped nuts, chocolate chips, oil, milk, egg and baking soda in large bowl with electric mixer at medium speed 2 minutes or until well blended. Pour into prepared pan.

3. Bake 30 to 35 minutes or until toothpick inserted into center comes out clean. Cool in pan on wire rack.

4. For topping, heat 1⅔ cups brown sugar and butter in medium saucepan; cook and stir over medium heat until smooth. Pour over cooled cake. Sprinkle with ½ cup chopped nuts.

BANANA SUPREME
⟶ CAKE ⟵

Makes 10 to 12 servings

1 package (about 15 ounces)
  yellow cake mix

1¼ cups water

3 eggs

⅓ cup vegetable oil

1 teaspoon vanilla

  Vanilla Cream Cheese Icing
  (recipe follows)

3 ripe bananas, sliced

1 cup lemon-lime soda

1 package (4-serving size)
  vanilla instant pudding
  and pie filling mix, plus
  ingredients to prepare mix

½ cup chopped walnuts
  (optional)

1. Preheat oven to 350ºF. Grease and flour two 9-inch round cake pans.

2. Beat cake mix, water, eggs, oil and vanilla in large bowl with electric mixer at medium speed until smooth. Pour batter into prepared pans. Bake 25 minutes or until toothpick inserted into centers comes out clean. Cool completely in pans on wire racks.

3. Prepare Vanilla Cream Cheese Icing. Soak sliced bananas in soda. Prepare pudding according to package directions in medium bowl. Beat until pudding begins to thicken.

4. Place one cake layer on serving plate. Top with half of pudding mixture. Arrange sliced bananas over top. Spoon remaining pudding over bananas. Top with remaining cake layer. Frost cake with Vanilla Cream Cheese Icing. Garnish with walnuts. Refrigerate until ready to serve.

VANILLA CREAM CHEESE ICING

Makes about 4 cups

2 containers (8 ounces each)
  whipped topping

1 package (8 ounces) cream
  cheese, softened

3 tablespoons boiling water

2 tablespoons powdered
  sugar

1 teaspoon vanilla

Beat all ingredients in large bowl with electric mixer at medium speed until creamy and smooth.

BREADS
AND MUFFINS

BANANA MONKEY BREAD

Makes 12 servings

2 ripe bananas

2 cups all-purpose flour, divided

¾ cup whole wheat flour

½ cup old-fashioned oats

¾ cup sugar, divided

¼ cup warm milk (120°F)

3 tablespoons vegetable or canola oil

1 package (¼ ounce) rapid-rise active dry yeast

1 teaspoon salt

2 teaspoons ground cinnamon, divided

5 tablespoons butter, melted and divided

1. Place bananas in large bowl. Beat with electric mixer at low speed 1 minute or until bananas are mashed. Add ¼ cup all-purpose flour, whole wheat flour, oats, ¼ cup sugar, milk, oil, yeast, salt and 1 teaspoon cinnamon. Beat at medium speed 3 minutes.

2. Beat in enough remaining all-purpose flour to form soft dough. Beat at low speed 5 minutes or until dough is smooth and elastic. Shape dough into a ball. Place in greased bowl; turn to grease top. Cover; let rise in warm place about 1 hour or until doubled in size.

3. Brush 12-cup (10-inch) bundt pan with 1 tablespoon butter. Place remaining 4 tablespoons butter in small bowl. Combine remaining ½ cup sugar and 1 teaspoon cinnamon in medium bowl. Turn out dough onto lightly floured surface; pat into 9-inch square. Cut into 1-inch squares; roll into balls. Dip balls in butter; roll in cinnamon-sugar to coat. Layer in prepared pan. Cover; let rise 1 hour until dough is puffy. Preheat oven to 350°F.

4. Bake 30 minutes or until bread is firm and golden brown. Loosen edges of bread with knife; immediately invert onto serving plate. Cool slightly before serving.

CHERRY BANANA
 BREAD

Makes 1 loaf, about 16 slices

1 (10-ounce) jar maraschino cherries

1¾ cups all-purpose flour

2 teaspoons baking powder

½ teaspoon salt

⅔ cup firmly packed brown sugar

⅓ cup butter or margarine, softened

2 eggs

1 cup mashed ripe bananas

½ cup chopped macadamia nuts or walnuts

Drain maraschino cherries, reserving 2 tablespoons juice. Cut cherries into quarters; set aside. Combine flour, baking powder and salt; set aside.

Combine brown sugar, butter, eggs and reserved cherry juice in a large bowl. Beat with an electric mixer at medium speed 3 to 4 minutes, or until well mixed. Add flour mixture and mashed bananas alternately, beginning and ending with flour mixture. Stir in drained cherries and nuts. Lightly spray a 9×5×3-inch baking pan with nonstick cooking spray. Spread batter evenly in pan.

Bake in a preheated 350°F oven 1 hour, or until golden brown and wooden pick inserted near center comes out clean. Remove from pan; let cool on wire rack. To store, wrap bread in plastic wrap.

Cherry Marketing Institute

BANANA DATE
BREAD

Prep Time: 20 minutes • Bake Time: 70 minutes, plus cooling

Makes 1 loaf or 12 servings

2 **cups flour**	½ **cup MAZOLA® Oil**
1½ **teaspoons baking powder**	1 **cup mashed ripe bananas**
¼ **teaspoon salt**	**(about 2 medium)**
2 **eggs**	1 **cup chopped dates**
⅔ **cup KARO® Light or Dark**	1 **cup chopped walnuts**
Corn Syrup	

1. Preheat oven to 375°F. Grease and flour 9×5×3-inch loaf pan. In medium bowl combine flour, baking powder and salt.

2. In large bowl with mixer at medium speed, beat eggs, corn syrup and oil until blended. Beat in bananas. Gradually stir in flour mixture just until moistened. Stir in dates and walnuts. Pour into prepared pan.

3. Bake 60 to 70 minutes or until toothpick inserted into center comes out clean. Cool in pan 10 minutes. Remove from pan; cool on wire rack.

BANANA & PEANUT BUTTER
MUFFINS

Prep Time: 12 minutes • Cook Time: 20 minutes
Makes 18 muffins

2⅓ **cups all-purpose flour**
1½ **teaspoons baking powder**
1 **teaspoon baking soda**
⅓ **cup SHEDD'S SPREAD COUNTRY CROCK® Spread**

¼ **cup SKIPPY® Creamy Peanut Butter**
½ **cup sugar**
2 **eggs**
1 **cup milk**
2 **ripe bananas, mashed**

1. Preheat oven to 400°F. Grease two 12-cup muffin pans or line with paper cupcake liners; set aside.

2. Combine flour, baking powder and baking soda in medium bowl; set aside.

3. Beat Spread with SKIPPY® Creamy Peanut Butter in large bowl, with electric mixer until smooth. Add sugar and beat until light and fluffy, about 3 minutes. Beat in eggs. Alternately beat in flour mixture and milk combined with bananas with mixer on low speed until blended. Evenly spoon batter into prepared pans to make 18 muffins, then carefully fill empty cups with water.

4. Bake 20 minutes or until toothpick inserted in centers comes out clean. Cool 10 minutes on wire rack; remove from pans and cool completely. Freeze leftover muffins individually for later use.

VARIATION: Try adding ⅓ cup mini chocolate chips or chopped walnuts for a simple twist.

APRICOT-BANANA-ALMOND ~ BREAD ~

Makes 1 loaf

2½ cups all-purpose flour, plus additional for dusting pan

1 cup QUAKER® Oats (quick or old fashioned, uncooked)

2 teaspoons baking powder

1 teaspoon baking soda

½ teaspoon salt

⅔ cup finely chopped dried apricots

¼ cup plus 2 tablespoons unblanched sliced almonds, divided

1 cup mashed ripe bananas (about 2 medium bananas)

½ cup low-fat buttermilk

⅓ cup vegetable oil

⅓ cup packed light brown sugar

2 eggs

¼ teaspoon almond extract

1. Heat oven to 350°F. Spray bottom only of 9×5-inch loaf pan with nonstick cooking spray. Coat bottom of pan with flour; tap out excess.

2. Combine flour, oats, baking powder, baking soda and salt in large bowl; mix well. Add apricots and ¼ cup almonds; mix well.

3. Whisk together bananas, buttermilk, oil, brown sugar, eggs and almond extract in medium bowl until well blended. Add to dry ingredients all at once; stir just until dry ingredients are evenly moistened. (Do not overmix.) Pour into pan. Sprinkle with remaining 2 tablespoons almonds.

4. Bake 55 to 65 minutes or until golden brown and wooden pick inserted in center comes out clean. Cool 10 minutes in pan on wire rack. Remove bread from pan. Cool completely on rack.

NOTE: To store, wrap covered bread tightly in aluminum foil and store up to 3 days at room temperature. For longer storage, label and freeze.

STRAWBERRY BANANA
BREAD

Preparation Time: 15 minutes • Bake Time: 55 minutes • Cooling Time: 30 minutes

Makes 16 servings

Nonstick cooking spray

1 cup oats

½ cup fat-free milk

1 cup mashed very
ripe bananas (about
2 medium)

½ cup cholesterol-free egg
substitute

½ cup canola oil

2 cups all-purpose flour

2 tablespoons sugar
substitute for baking
or ¼ cup sugar

2 teaspoons baking powder

½ teaspoon baking soda

½ teaspoon salt

½ cup POLANER® Sugar Free
Strawberry or Sugar Free
Blueberry Preserves

Heat oven to 350°F. Lightly coat bottom only of 8×4-inch loaf pan with nonstick cooking spray.

Combine oats and milk in medium bowl; mix well. Let stand 10 minutes. Stir in bananas, egg substitute and oil until combined.

Combine flour, sugar substitute, baking powder, baking soda and salt in large bowl; mix well. Add banana mixture to dry ingredients all at once; stir just until ingredients are moistened.

Stir preserves in small bowl until thinned to spreading consistency.

Pour half of batter into prepared pan. Spoon preserves over batter, spreading to cover. Spoon remaining batter evenly over preserves.

Bake 55 to 60 minutes or until wooden pick inserted in center comes out clean. Cool in pan on wire rack 10 minutes. Remove from pan. Cool completely.

TIP: Store banana bread, tightly wrapped in plastic wrap or foil, at room temperature. Freeze for longer storage.

TIP: This special banana bread makes a great hostess gift. Wrap in decorative foil or colored plastic wrap, tuck in a basket or onto a cutting board and add a jar of preserves.

⸻ HEARTY ⸻
BANANA CARROT MUFFINS

Prep Time: 20 minutes • Bake Time: 14 minutes

Makes 12 muffins

2 **ripe, medium DOLE®
    Bananas**

1 **package (14 ounces) oat
    bran muffin mix**

¾ **teaspoon ground ginger**

1 **medium DOLE® Carrot,
    shredded (½ cup)**

⅓ **cup light molasses**

⅓ **cup DOLE® Seedless or
    Golden Raisins**

¼ **cup chopped almonds**

1. MASH bananas with fork (1 cup).

2. COMBINE muffin mix and ginger in large bowl. Add carrot, molasses, raisins and bananas. Stir just until moistened.

3. SPOON batter into paper-lined muffin cups. Sprinkle tops with almonds.

4. BAKE at 425°F 12 to 14 minutes or until browned.

BANANA BRAN BREAD

Makes 9 slices

1 cup bran cereal

½ cup boiling water

1⅓ cups all-purpose flour

½ cup sugar

1 teaspoon baking powder

½ teaspoon baking soda

¼ to ¾ teaspoon salt

¼ teaspoon ground cinnamon

2 tablespoons vegetable oil

2 eggs

1 cup mashed ripe bananas (2 medium to large)

¼ cup crumbled unsweetened banana chips

1. Preheat oven to 350°F. Spray 8×4-inch loaf pan with nonstick cooking spray.

2. Place cereal into medium bowl; stir in boiling water. Let stand 10 minutes. Combine flour, sugar, baking powder, baking soda, salt and cinnamon in large bowl. Whisk oil and eggs in small bowl; add to flour mixture. Stir in bran mixture and mashed bananas. Spoon batter into prepared pan. Sprinkle with banana chips.

3. Bake 45 to 50 minutes or until toothpick inserted into center comes out clean. Cool in pan 5 minutes. Remove to wire rack; cool completely.

BANANA CHOCOLATE MINI MUFFINS

Makes 36 mini muffins

2¼ **cups all-purpose flour**	½ **cup (1 stick) butter, melted**
1 **cup packed brown sugar**	2 **eggs**
2 **teaspoons baking powder**	½ **teaspoon vanilla**
½ **teaspoon salt**	1 **cup mini chocolate-coated**
1 **cup mashed ripe bananas**	**candy pieces or mini**
(about 2 large)	**chocolate chips**

1. Preheat oven to 350°F. Spray 36 mini (1¾-inch) muffin cups with nonstick cooking spray or line with paper baking cups.

2. Combine flour, brown sugar, baking powder and salt in large bowl; mix well. Beat bananas, butter, eggs and vanilla in medium bowl until well blended. Add banana mixture and candy pieces to flour mixture; stir just until moistened. Spoon batter into prepared muffin cups, filling almost full.

3. Bake 15 minutes or until tops are golden brown and toothpick inserted into centers comes out clean. Cool in pans on wire racks 5 minutes. Remove from pans; cool completely on wire racks.

BLACK FOREST BANANA BREAD

Makes 1 loaf

1 jar (10 ounces) maraschino cherries

1¾ cups all-purpose flour

2 teaspoons baking powder

½ teaspoon salt

⅔ cup packed brown sugar

⅓ cup butter, softened

1 cup mashed ripe bananas (about 2 large)

2 eggs

1 cup semisweet chocolate chips

¾ cup chopped pecans

1. Preheat oven to 350°F. Lightly spray 9×5-inch loaf pan with nonstick cooking spray. Drain cherries, reserving 2 tablespoons juice. Coarsely chop cherries.

2. Combine flour, baking powder and salt in medium bowl. Beat brown sugar and butter in large bowl with electric mixer until creamy. Beat in bananas, eggs and reserved cherry juice until well blended. Stir in flour mixture, chopped cherries, chocolate chips and pecans just until blended. Pour into prepared pan.

3. Bake 1 hour or until golden brown and toothpick inserted into center comes out clean. Cool in pan on wire rack 10 minutes. Remove bread from pan; cool completely on wire rack.

BANANA PEANUT BUTTER CHIP MUFFINS

Makes 15 muffins

2 cups all-purpose flour	½ cup (1 stick) butter, melted
¾ cup sugar	2 eggs, beaten
2 teaspoons baking powder	⅓ cup buttermilk
½ teaspoon baking soda	1½ teaspoons vanilla
¼ teaspoon salt	1 cup peanut butter chips
1 cup mashed ripe bananas (about 2 large)	½ cup chopped peanuts

1. Preheat oven to 375°F. Grease 15 standard (2½-inch) muffins cups or line with paper baking cups.

2. Combine flour, sugar, baking powder, baking soda and salt in large bowl. Beat bananas, butter, eggs, buttermilk and vanilla in medium bowl until well blended.

3. Add banana mixture to flour mixture; stir just until blended. Gently fold in peanut butter chips. Spoon batter into prepared muffin cups, filling three-fourths full. Sprinkle with chopped peanuts.

4. Bake 20 minutes or until toothpick inserted into centers comes out clean. Cool in pans 2 minutes. Remove to wire racks; cool completely.

VARIATION: Substitute a mixture of chocolate and peanut butter chips for the peanut butter chips for a combination of three great flavors in one muffin.

BANANA-PECAN BREAD

Makes 1 loaf (about 16 servings)

3 large ripe bananas, mashed (about 1⅓ cups)

½ cup packed dark brown sugar

¼ cup granulated sugar

2 eggs, lightly beaten

¼ cup milk

¼ cup canola oil

2 cups biscuit baking mix

1 teaspoon ground cinnamon

½ cup golden raisins

½ cup chopped pecans

1. Preheat oven to 350°F. Spray 9×5-inch loaf pan with nonstick cooking spray. Lightly dust with flour.

2. Combine bananas, brown sugar, granulated sugar, eggs, milk and oil in large bowl; gently stir until combined. Stir in baking mix and cinnamon until well blended. Fold in raisins and pecans. Pour into prepared pan.

3. Bake 45 to 50 minutes or until top is golden brown and toothpick inserted into center comes out clean. Cool in pan on wire rack 20 minutes. Remove to wire rack; serve warm or cool completely.

COOL
TREATS

TROPICAL SMOOTHIE
PUNCH

Makes about 1 gallon

1 can (46 oz.) DOLE®
Pineapple Juice, chilled,
divided

1 pkg. (12 oz.) DOLE® Frozen
Raspberries, partially
thawed, divided

4 cups *or* 1 liter sugar-free
lemon-lime soda, chilled

½ can (12 oz.) frozen limeade
concentrate, thawed

1 pkg. (16 oz.) DOLE® Frozen
Sliced Peaches, partially
thawed

2 DOLE® Bananas, peeled,
sliced

2 oranges, peeled, sliced

1. COMBINE 1½ cups pineapple juice and ½ of the raspberries in blender container. Cover; blend until smooth.

2. COMBINE all remaining ingredients in punch bowl. Stir to combine.

BANANA FREEZER POPS

Makes 8 servings

2 ripe medium bananas

1 can (6 ounces) frozen
orange juice concentrate

¼ cup water

1 tablespoon honey

1 teaspoon vanilla

8 (3-ounce) paper or plastic
cups

8 wooden sticks

1. Place bananas, orange juice concentrate, water, honey and vanilla in blender or food processor; blend until smooth.

2. Pour banana mixture evenly into cups. Cover top of each cup with small piece of foil. Insert wooden stick through center of foil into banana mixture.

3. Place cups on tray; freeze until firm. Remove foil and cups before serving.

PEPPY PURPLE POPS: Omit honey and vanilla. Substitute grape juice concentrate for orange juice concentrate.

Banana Freezer Pops

FROZEN CHOCOLATE BANANA POPS

Makes 6 servings

3 **bananas,* peeled**

6 **ice cream sticks or wooden skewers**

½ **cup semisweet chocolate chips**

1½ **teaspoons vegetable oil**

¼ **cup sprinkles, chopped peanuts, coconut or crushed cookies (optional)**

You may substitute 6 baby bananas.

1. Line baking sheet with waxed paper or foil. Cut each banana in half. Insert ice cream stick halfway into each banana. Place on prepared baking sheet; freeze 1 hour.

2. Combine chocolate chips and oil in small saucepan; stir over low heat until melted and smooth. Place toppings on individual plates, if using.

3. Remove bananas from freezer. Spoon chocolate over each banana while holding over saucepan. Roll in toppings to coat. Return to baking sheet; freeze about 1 hour or until chocolate and toppings are set. Store in airtight container or resealable freezer food storage bag.

NOTE: If desired, bananas can be cut into 1-inch pieces, frozen, then dipped in chocolate for individual bites.

FRUIT SALAD WITH CREAMY BANANA DRESSING

Makes 8 servings

2 **cups fresh pineapple chunks**

1 **cup cantaloupe cubes**

1 **cup honeydew melon cubes**

1 **cup fresh blackberries**

1 **cup sliced fresh strawberries**

1 **cup seedless red grapes**

1 **medium apple, diced**

2 **medium ripe bananas, sliced**

½ **cup vanilla nonfat Greek yogurt**

2 **tablespoons honey**

1 **tablespoon lemon juice**

¼ **teaspoon ground nutmeg**

1. Combine pineapple, cantaloupe, honeydew, blackberries, strawberries, grapes and apple in large bowl; gently mix.

2. Combine bananas, yogurt, honey, lemon juice and nutmeg in blender or food processor; blend until smooth.

3. Pour dressing over fruit mixture; gently toss to coat evenly. Serve immediately.

TIP: There are hundreds of varieties of bananas. The most common one in American supermarkets is the yellow Cavendish. Some larger supermarkets carry such varieties as the short, chunky red banana and the tiny finger banana; both are known for their sweetness. Plantains are large, firm bananas with rough skins and a squash like flavor. They are a staple food in the tropics where they are used as a starchy vegetable but never eaten raw.

CHOCOLATE AND BANANA
CREAM LAYERED PIE

Makes 7 to 8 servings

Graham Cracker Crust (recipe follows)

3 tablespoons cornstarch

½ teaspoon salt

1 cup cold water

1 can (14 ounces) sweetened condensed milk

4 egg yolks, beaten

⅓ cup plus 1 tablespoon half-and-half, divided

1 tablespoon unsalted butter

1½ teaspoons vanilla

1 square (1 ounce) unsweetened chocolate, finely chopped

2 medium bananas, divided

½ cup whipped topping, plus additional for topping

Grated semisweet chocolate (optional)

1. Preheat oven to 375°F. Prepare Graham Cracker Crust. Bake 7 to 8 minutes. Cool on wire rack.

2. Combine cornstarch and salt in medium saucepan. Stir in water until cornstarch dissolves. Stir in sweetened condensed milk, egg yolks and ⅓ cup half-and-half; bring to a boil over medium heat. Cook about 8 minutes, stirring constantly. Remove from heat; stir in butter and vanilla.

3. Measure out 1 cup hot filling and place in small bowl. Stir in chocolate and remaining 1 tablespoon half-and-half until blended. Cool slightly, then spread chocolate filling on bottom of crust. Refrigerate. Transfer vanilla filling to medium bowl; cover with plastic wrap and refrigerate 1 hour.

4. Cut one banana crosswise into ¼-inch slices; arrange over chocolate filling. Fold ½ cup whipped topping into vanilla filling; pour filling over banana slices. Cover with plastic wrap and refrigerate at least 3 hours.

5. Spread pie with additional whipped topping. Slice remaining banana; garnish pie with banana slices and grated chocolate.

GRAHAM CRACKER CRUST: Combine 1¼ cups graham cracker crumbs, 3 tablespoons sugar and ⅓ cup melted unsalted butter in medium bowl. Mix with fork until blended. Press mixture into 9-inch pie pan.

BANANA PRALINE
⎯⎯ ICE CREAM CAKE ⎯⎯

Makes 12 servings

1 package (about 18 ounces) German chocolate cake mix

1⅓ cups water

3 eggs

⅓ cup vegetable oil

2 ripe medium bananas, mashed*

2 cups chopped pecans

½ cup (1 stick) butter

½ cup firmly packed dark brown sugar

2 teaspoons ground cinnamon

2 cups vanilla ice cream, slightly softened

¼ cup caramel ice cream topping

1 ripe medium banana, sliced

*Do not use overripe bananas.

1. Preheat oven to 325°F. Coat 2 (8-inch) round cake pans with nonstick cooking spray.

2. Combine cake mix, water, eggs, oil and 2 mashed bananas in large bowl; beat according to package directions. Divide batter evenly between prepared pans. Bake 33 to 35 minutes or until toothpick inserted into centers comes out clean. Cool 15 minutes in pans on wire rack. Invert onto wire rack to cool completely. (For easier assembly, wrap layers in plastic wrap; freeze overnight.)

3. Heat large nonstick skillet over medium-high heat. Add pecans; cook and stir 2 minutes or until pecans begin to lightly brown. Add butter, brown sugar and cinnamon; cook and stir until butter has just melted. Remove from heat; cool completely. Reserve ½ cup praline pecans; set aside.

4. Place one cake layer on serving platter. Working quickly, spoon ice cream evenly over cake. Sprinkle evenly with 1½ cups praline pecans. Place remaining cake layer on top. Spread caramel topping evenly on top layer. Arrange banana slices on caramel topping; sprinkle evenly with reserved ½ cup praline pecans. Freeze overnight or until firm. Allow cake to stand a few minutes before slicing.

TIP: Prepare the ice cream layer in advance. Line an 8-inch round cake pan with plastic wrap. Fill the pan with ice cream. Freeze 1 to 2 hours or until firm. Using the plastic wrap, pop the ice cream layer out of the pan. If you need the pan for baking, place the wrapped ice cream round in the freezer until you're ready to assemble the cake.

COOL GELATIN
DESSERT

Makes 12 servings

2 **cups water**

1 **package (4-serving size) strawberry gelatin**

1 **pound (16 ounces) fresh strawberries or thawed frozen unsweetened strawberries**

3 **mashed bananas**

1 **can (16 ounces) crushed pineapple in juice, drained**

1 **pint sour cream**

Sprigs fresh mint (optional)

1. Bring water to a boil in large saucepan. Add gelatin; stir until gelatin completely dissolves. Add strawberries, bananas and pineapple; stir gently until well combined.

2. Remove from heat. Pour mixture into 8-inch square pan; refrigerate 4 hours or until firm. Cut into 12 squares. Top with dollop of sour cream and garnish with mint before serving.

VARIATION: Instead of sour cream, you may also top with a dollop of vanilla yogurt.

BANANA SPLIT ICE CREAM SANDWICHES

Makes 9 servings

1 package (about 16 ounces) refrigerated chocolate chip cookie dough	**4 cups strawberry ice cream, softened**
2 ripe bananas, mashed	**Hot fudge topping**
½ cup strawberry jam	**Whipped cream**
	9 maraschino cherries

1. Let dough stand at room temperature about 15 minutes. Preheat oven to 350°F. Lightly grease 13×9-inch baking pan.

2. Beat dough and bananas in large bowl with electric mixer at medium speed until well blended. Spread dough evenly in prepared pan; smooth top. Bake 22 minutes or until edges are light brown. Cool completely in pan on wire rack.

3. Line 8-inch square baking pan with foil or plastic wrap, allowing some to hang over edges of pan. Remove cooled cookie from pan; cut in half crosswise. Place 1 cookie half, top side down, in 8-inch pan, trimming edges to fit, if necessary. Spread ¼ cup jam evenly over cookie. Spread ice cream evenly over jam. Spread remaining ¼ cup jam over bottom of remaining cookie half; place jam side down over ice cream. Wrap tightly with foil; freeze 2 hours or overnight.

4. Cut into bars and top with hot fudge topping, whipped cream and cherries.

BANANA PUDDING
SQUARES

Makes 18 servings

1 cup graham cracker crumbs

2 tablespoons butter, melted

1 package (8 ounces) cream cheese, softened

3 cups milk

2 packages (4-serving size each) banana cream instant pudding and pie filling mix

1 container (8 ounces) whipped topping, divided

2 medium bananas

1. Line 13×9-inch baking pan with foil; spray with nonstick cooking spray.

2. Combine graham cracker crumbs and butter in small bowl; stir until well blended. Press into bottom of prepared pan.

3. Beat cream cheese in large bowl with electric mixer at low speed until smooth. Add milk and pudding mixes; beat at high speed 2 minutes or until smooth and creamy. Fold in half of whipped topping until well blended. Reserve half of pudding mixture. Spread remaining pudding mixture over crust.

4. Peel bananas; cut into ¼-inch slices. Arrange bananas evenly over pudding layer. Spoon reserved pudding mixture over bananas; spread remaining whipped topping evenly over pudding mixture.

5. Cover loosely with plastic wrap; refrigerate 2 hours or up to 8 hours.

EASY
STRAWBERRY MOUSSE PIE

Prep Time: 30 minutes • Chill Time: 4 hours

Makes 8 servings

1 cup boiling water

1 package (4-serving size) strawberry gelatin

2 extra ripe, medium DOLE® Bananas

1 carton (6 ounces) strawberry yogurt

2 cups thawed whipped topping

1 cup DOLE® Frozen Whole or Sliced Strawberries, partially thawed, quartered or sliced

1 (9-inch) prepared pie crust

1. STIR boiling water into gelatin in medium bowl at least 2 minutes until completely dissolved. Place in freezer about 20 minutes or until slightly thickened, stirring occasionally.

2. PLACE bananas in blender or food processor container. Cover; blend until smooth.

3. COMBINE yogurt and puréed bananas in large bowl. Blend gelatin mixture into banana mixture. Refrigerate until slightly thickened. Fold whipped topping into gelatin mixture with strawberries.

4. SPOON gelatin mixture into prepared crust. Refrigerate 4 hours or until firm. Garnish with additional whipped topping and strawberries, if desired.

Bananas Foster Freeze

BANANAS FOSTER FREEZE

Makes 4 servings

5 bananas	¼ teaspoon ground cinnamon, plus additional for garnish
¾ cup plain yogurt	¼ teaspoon ground cloves
½ cup vanilla frozen yogurt	¼ teaspoon ground nutmeg
¼ cup cold whole milk	2 bananas, halved (optional)
¼ cup packed brown sugar, plus additional for garnish	

1. Place 5 bananas, plain yogurt, frozen yogurt, milk, ¼ cup brown sugar, ¼ teaspoon cinnamon, cloves and nutmeg in blender; blend until smooth.

2. Pour into 4 glasses. Garnish with banana halves. Sprinkle with additional brown sugar and cinnamon. Serve immediately.

WATERMELON BANANA SPLIT

Makes 4 servings

2 bananas	1 cup sliced fresh strawberries
1 medium watermelon	
1 cup fresh blueberries	¼ cup caramel fruit dip
1 cup diced fresh pineapple	¼ cup honey roasted almonds

Peel bananas and cut in half lengthwise then cut each piece in half. For each serving, lay 2 banana pieces against sides of shallow dish. Using an ice cream scooper, place three watermelon "scoops" in between each banana in each dish. Remove seeds if necessary. Top each watermelon "scoop" with a different fresh fruit topping. Drizzle caramel fruit dip over all. Sprinkle with almonds.

National Watermelon Promotion Board

CHOCOLATE BANANA SPLIT DESSERT

Makes 16 servings

22 ounces **KOZY SHACK®** *No Sugar Added* **Chocolate Pudding**

14 ounces **sugar-free shortbread cookies**

⅓ cup **trans fat-free margarine, melted**

4 ounces **⅓ fat cream cheese**

1 teaspoon **vanilla extract**

3 medium-sized **bananas, sliced**

6 ounces **fresh strawberries, sliced**

16 **maraschino cherries**

½ cup **chopped nuts (pecans or walnuts)**

¼ cup **sugar-free chocolate syrup (optional)**

1. Combine crushed cookies with margarine.

2. Layer the bottom of a 13×9-pan with cookie mixture.

3. In a mixing bowl, whip cream cheese and vanilla extract.

4. Slowly whip the chocolate pudding into the mixture.

5. Spread the chocolate cream cheese mixture over the crust.

6. Cover and chill in refrigerator for 30 minutes.

7. Place bananas, strawberries and cherries over the pudding. Sprinkle with nuts; drizzle with syrup, if desired.

STRAWBERRY-BANANA GRANITÉ

Makes 5 servings

2 **ripe medium bananas, peeled and sliced (about 2 cups)**

2 **cups unsweetened frozen strawberries (do not thaw)**

¼ **cup strawberry pourable fruit***

Sprigs fresh mint (optional)

Or substitute 3 tablespoons strawberry fruit spread combined with 1 tablespoon warm water.

1. Place banana slices in resealable freezer food storage bag; freeze until firm.

2. Combine bananas and strawberries in food processor or blender; let stand 10 minutes to soften slightly.

3. Add pourable fruit to food processor. Remove plunger from top of food processor to allow air to be incorporated. Process until smooth, scraping down side of bowl frequently. Garnish with mint, if desired. Serve immediately.

TIP: Granité can be transferred to airtight container and frozen up to 1 month. Let stand at room temperature 10 minutes to soften slightly before serving.

BANANA
FAVORITES

BANANA OATMEAL COOKIES

Makes about 2 dozen cookies

1 cup raisins	1 teaspoon salt
5 tablespoons boiling water	1½ cups sugar
2 cups quick oats	¾ cup shortening
2 cups all-purpose flour	2 eggs
1 tablespoon ground cinnamon	3 bananas, mashed
1 tablespoon apple pie spice	¼ cup milk
1 teaspoon baking soda	½ cup chopped pecans

1. Preheat oven to 375°F. Place raisins in small bowl. Pour boiling water over raisins; set aside.

2. Combine oats, flour, cinnamon, apple pie spice, baking soda and salt in separate bowl. Beat sugar and shortening in large bowl with electric mixer at medium speed until creamy. Add eggs, one at a time, beating well after each addition. Add bananas and milk, beating until fluffy. Gradually add oats mixture to sugar mixture; beat on low speed until stiff dough forms. Stir in raisins and pecans.

3. Drop by heaping tablespoonfuls 2 inches apart on ungreased cookie sheets. Bake 12 to 15 minutes or until light brown and edges are set. Cool on cookie sheets 1 minute. Remove to wire racks; cool completely.

GRILLED FRUIT & POUND CAKE

Prep Time: 15 minutes • Grill Time: 4 minutes

Makes 4 servings

REYNOLDS WRAP®
Non-Stick Foil

½ **cup honey**

¼ **cup (½ stick) butter, melted**

½ **teaspoon ground cinnamon**

8 **slices pound cake, ½-inch thick**

4 **fresh peaches, peeled and halved**

4 **fresh pineapple slices, ½-inch thick**

2 **fresh bananas, quartered**

Fresh strawberries, hulled and halved

1 **jar (11.75 ounces) hot fudge ice cream topping, heated**

Combine honey, butter and cinnamon; set aside.

Preheat grill to medium-high. Make holes in a sheet of REYNOLDS WRAP® Non-Stick Foil with a large grilling fork.

Brush one side of cake slices with honey mixture.

Place foil sheet with holes on grill grate with non-stick (dull) side toward food. Immediately arrange cake slices brushed-side down on foil. Grill 2 minutes in covered grill. Brush tops with honey mixture; turn. Grill 2 minutes longer or until lightly browned. Remove cake from foil.

Brush one side of peaches, pineapple and bananas with honey mixture; arrange brushed-side down, on foil. Grill 4 minutes in covered grill. Brush tops with honey mixture; turn. Grill 3 to 4 minutes longer or until lightly browned. Remove fruit from foil. Garnish with strawberries; drizzle with hot fudge topping before serving.

BANANAS FOSTER
CRISP

Makes 8 to 10 servings

¾ cup packed dark brown sugar, divided

6 tablespoons (¾ stick) butter, divided

3 tablespoons dark rum

½ teaspoon ground cinnamon

¼ teaspoon grated nutmeg

8 medium bananas (firm, yellow, no spots), cut into ½-inch slices (about 6 cups)

½ cup all-purpose flour

½ cup chopped pecans

¼ teaspoon salt

Vanilla ice cream (optional)

1. Place oven rack in lower-middle position. Preheat oven to 375°F. Spray 8-inch round or square baking dish with nonstick cooking spray.

2. Combine ½ cup brown sugar and 2 tablespoons butter in small saucepan; cook and stir over medium heat about 3 minutes or until butter has melted and sugar has dissolved. Slowly add rum, cinnamon and nutmeg (mixture will spatter); cook 1 minute, stirring constantly. Pour mixture into large bowl. Add bananas; toss to coat. Spoon into prepared baking dish.

3. Combine flour, pecans, remaining ¼ cup brown sugar and salt in medium bowl; mix well. Cut remaining 4 tablespoons butter into small pieces. Add to flour mixture; mix with fingertips until mixture forms coarse crumbs. Sprinkle over banana mixture.

4. Bake 40 minutes or until filling is bubbly and topping is golden brown. Let stand 1 hour before serving. Serve with ice cream, if desired.

BANANA-HAZELNUT WHOOPIE PIES

Makes 20 whoopie pies

COOKIES

- 2 cups all-purpose flour
- 1 teaspoon salt
- 1 teaspoon ground cinnamon
- ½ teaspoon baking soda
- ½ teaspoon baking powder
- ½ cup (1 stick) butter, softened
- ½ cup granulated sugar
- ½ cup packed dark brown sugar
- 1 egg
- 1½ teaspoons vanilla
- 1 cup mashed ripe bananas (about 2 medium)
- ½ cup sour cream

FILLING

- ⅔ cup chocolate-hazelnut spread
- ½ cup (1 stick) butter, softened
- 1 cup powdered sugar
- 1½ tablespoons whipping cream
- 1 teaspoon vanilla

1. For cookies, preheat oven to 350°F. Line two cookie sheets with parchment paper. Sift flour, salt, cinnamon, baking soda and baking powder into medium bowl.

2. Beat ½ cup butter, granulated sugar and brown sugar in large bowl with electric mixer at medium speed 5 minutes or until light and fluffy. Beat in egg and 1½ teaspoons vanilla. Add bananas and sour cream; beat at low speed until blended. Beat in flour mixture until combined. Drop rounded tablespoonfuls of batter 2 inches apart onto prepared cookie sheets.

3. Bake 10 to 12 minutes or until cookies spring back when lightly touched. Cool 2 minutes on cookie sheets. Remove to wire racks; cool completely.

4. For filling, beat chocolate-hazelnut spread and ½ cup butter in large bowl with electric mixer at medium speed until smooth. Add powdered sugar, cream and 1 teaspoon vanilla; beat until smooth.

5. Pipe or spread 2 tablespoons filling on flat side of half of cookies; top with remaining cookies.

DARK CHOCOLATE BANANA CUPCAKES

Makes 18 cupcakes

1½ cups all-purpose flour

1½ cups granulated sugar

½ cup unsweetened Dutch process cocoa powder

2 tablespoons packed brown sugar

2 teaspoons baking powder

½ teaspoon salt

½ cup vegetable oil

2 eggs

¼ cup buttermilk

1 teaspoon vanilla

2 mashed bananas (about 1 cup)

1½ cups whipping cream

2 cups dark chocolate chips

Dried banana chips (optional)

1. Preheat oven to 350°F. Line 18 standard (2½-inch) muffin cups with paper baking cups.

2. Whisk flour, granulated sugar, cocoa, brown sugar, baking powder and salt in large bowl. Add oil, eggs, buttermilk and vanilla; beat with electric mixer at medium speed 2 minutes or until well blended. Beat in bananas until well blended. Spoon batter into prepared muffin cups, filling three-fourths full.

3. Bake 25 minutes or until toothpick inserted into centers comes out clean. Cool in pans 10 minutes. Remove to wire racks; cool completely.

4. Bring cream to a simmer in small saucepan over medium heat. Place chocolate chips in medium heatproof bowl. Pour cream over chocolate chips; let stand 2 minutes. Whisk mixture until chocolate is melted and mixture is smooth.

5. Dip tops of cupcakes in chocolate mixture; return to wire racks. Let stand 10 minutes; dip tops again, if desired. Drizzle banana chips with remaining chocolate mixture; arrange on cupcakes, if desired.

COCOA BOTTOM BANANA PECAN BARS

Makes 2 dozen bars

1 **cup sugar**	1 **teaspoon baking powder**
½ **cup (1 stick) butter**	1 **teaspoon baking soda**
5 **ripe bananas, mashed**	½ **teaspoon salt**
1 **egg**	½ **cup chopped pecans**
1 **teaspoon vanilla**	¼ **cup unsweetened cocoa**
1½ **cups all-purpose flour**	**powder**

1. Preheat oven to 350°F. Grease 13×9-inch baking pan.

2. Beat sugar and butter in large bowl with electric mixer at medium speed until creamy. Add bananas, egg and vanilla; beat until well blended. Combine flour, baking powder, baking soda and salt in medium bowl. Add to banana mixture; beat until well blended. Stir in pecans.

3. Remove half of batter to another bowl; stir in cocoa. Spread chocolate batter in prepared pan. Top with plain batter; swirl gently with knife.

4. Bake 30 to 35 minutes or until edges are lightly browned. Cool completely in pan on wire rack. Cut into bars.

*Grilled Banana and
Chocolate Panini*

GRILLED BANANA AND CHOCOLATE PANINI

Prep Time: 10 minutes • Cook Time: 10 minutes

Makes 6 servings

¼ cup (½ stick) butter, softened

1 frozen pound cake (about 10 ounces), thawed and cut into 12 (½-inch-thick) slices

1 cup chocolate-hazelnut spread

3 ripe bananas, cut lengthwise into slices

Ground cinnamon

1. Lightly butter one side of each pound cake slice; set aside.

2. For each panini, lay one slice pound cake, buttered side down, on work surface. Spread with about 1 tablespoon chocolate-hazelnut spread; top with banana slices and sprinkle with cinnamon. Top with second slice pound cake, buttered side up.

3. Spray indoor grill with nonstick cooking spray; heat to medium. Cook 2 minutes or until pound cake is golden brown.

BANANAS FOSTER

Prep Time: 5 minutes • Cook Time: 5 minutes

Makes 4 servings

6 tablespoons I CAN'T BELIEVE IT'S NOT BUTTER!® Spread

3 tablespoons firmly packed brown sugar

4 ripe medium bananas, sliced diagonally

2 tablespoons dark rum or brandy (optional)

Vanilla ice cream

In 12-inch skillet, bring I Can't Believe It's Not Butter!® Spread, brown sugar and bananas to a boil. Cook 2 minutes, stirring gently. Carefully add rum to center of pan and cook 15 seconds. Serve hot banana mixture over scoops of ice cream and top, if desired, with sweetened whipped cream.

BANANA CREAM PIE
⌒ CUPCAKES ⌒

Makes 24 cupcakes

1 **package (about 15 ounces) yellow cake mix, plus ingredients to prepare mix**

1 **package (4-serving size) banana instant pudding and pie filling mix**

2 **cups milk**

2 **bananas**

2 **tablespoons sugar, divided**

2 **cups whipping cream**

1. Preheat oven to 350°F. Line 24 standard (2½-inch) muffin cups with paper baking cups. Prepare cake mix according to package directions. Spoon batter evenly into prepared muffin cups.

2. Bake 20 minutes or until toothpick inserted into centers comes out clean. Cool in pans 10 minutes. Remove to wire racks; cool completely.

3. Prepare pudding using milk according to package directions. Cover and refrigerate until set.

4. Preheat broiler. Line baking sheet with parchment paper. Cut each banana into 12 slices. Place 1 tablespoon sugar in shallow bowl. Dip one side each of banana slice into sugar; place sugar side up on prepared baking sheet. Broil 2 minutes or until golden brown. Cool completely.

5. Beat cream and remaining 1 tablespoon sugar in large bowl with electric mixer at medium-high speed until stiff peaks form.

6. Cut 1-inch hole in tops of cupcakes; discard cupcake pieces. Fill holes with pudding (reserve remaining pudding for another use). Place whipped cream in piping bag fitted with large star tip; pipe whipped cream over filling. Top each cupcake with banana slice.

CINNAMON-SUGAR TRIANGLES ⌒WITH⌒ CARAMELIZED BANANAS

Makes 4 servings

2 **pocketless pita-style round flatbreads**

2 **tablespoons melted unsalted butter**

1 **tablespoon granulated sugar**

¼ **teaspoon ground cinnamon**

1 **tablespoon packed brown sugar**

⅛ **teaspoon salt**

1 **large banana, cut into ⅛-inch-thick slices**

Vanilla ice cream (optional)

1. Brush both sides of flatbread with butter (you will not use it all). Combine granulated sugar and cinnamon in small bowl; sprinkle over one side of each flatbread.

2. Heat large nonstick skillet over medium-high heat. Working one at a time, place flatbread in skillet, cinnamon-sugar side up; cook 1 to 2 minutes or until bottom is golden brown and crisp. Turn and cook 1 minute until sugar is caramelized but not burned. Transfer to cutting board.

3. Reduce heat to medium, add remaining butter, brown sugar and salt. Cook 30 seconds until mixture is blended. Add banana; cook 1 minute until tender. Pour half of bananas over each flatbread; cut each flatbread into six wedges. Serve with ice cream, if desired.

Makes 30 cupcakes

1 **package (about 18 ounces) yellow cake mix, divided**

1 **cup water**

1 **cup mashed ripe bananas**

3 **eggs**

1 **cup chopped drained maraschino cherries**

1½ **cups mini semisweet chocolate chips, divided**

1½ **cups prepared vanilla frosting**

1 **cup marshmallow creme**

1 **teaspoon shortening**

30 **whole maraschino cherries, drained and patted dry**

1. Preheat oven to 350°F. Line 30 standard (2½-inch) muffin cups with paper baking cups.

2. Reserve 2 tablespoons cake mix. Beat remaining cake mix, water, bananas and eggs in large bowl with electric mixer at low speed 30 seconds or until moistened. Beat at medium speed 2 minutes. Combine chopped cherries and reserved 2 tablespoons cake mix in small bowl. Stir chopped cherry mixture and 1 cup chocolate chips into batter. Spoon batter into prepared muffin cups, filling two-thirds full.

3. Bake 15 to 20 minutes or until toothpick inserted into centers comes out clean. Cool in pans 10 minutes. Remove to wire racks; cool completely.

4. Combine frosting and marshmallow creme in medium bowl until well blended. Frost cupcakes.

5. Combine remaining ½ cup chocolate chips and shortening in small microwavable bowl. Microwave on HIGH 30 to 45 seconds or until melted and smooth, stirring after 30 seconds. Drizzle chocolate mixture over cupcakes. Place 1 whole cherry on each cupcake.

NOTE: If desired, omit chocolate drizzle and top cupcakes with colored sprinkles.

BANANA-CHOCOLATE BREAD PUDDING WITH CREAM

Makes 8 servings

BREAD PUDDING

- **1 (1-pound) unsliced loaf cinnamon-swirl bread, cut into 1-inch cubes***
- **2 packages (3.4 ounces each) chocolate pudding mix (not instant)**
- **3½ cups whole milk**
- **½ cup (1 stick) butter, melted**
- **2 bananas**

CREAM

- **1 cup crème fraîche**
- **2 tablespoons powdered sugar**
- **¼ cup whipping cream**

GARNISH

- **Powdered sugar**
- **16 strawberries, sliced**
- **Sprigs fresh mint (optional)**

1. Preheat oven to 400°F. Spread bread pieces on large baking sheet; toast in oven 5 to 10 minutes or until light brown. Set aside to cool.

2. *Reduce oven temperature to 350°F.* Spray 8 (1-cup) custard cups with nonstick cooking spray.

3. For bread pudding, blend pudding mixes and milk in large bowl; stir until smooth. Stir in butter. Add bread cubes; toss gently. Let mixture stand 10 to 15 minutes to allow bread to absorb custard, stirring gently every few minutes to coat bread completely. Cut bananas into ½-inch slices; stir into bread cube mixture. Divide mixture among custard cups. Transfer to baking sheet; bake 45 to 50 minutes or until set in center. Let cool slightly.

4. For cream, fold together crème fraîche, 2 tablespoons powdered sugar and whipping cream.

5. To serve, dust serving plates with powdered sugar. Remove puddings from custard cups; place on serving plates. Top with sliced strawberries. Spoon cream on top. Garnish with mint.

NOTE: Crème fraîche is produced from heavy cream allowed to ferment with a special culture. Crème fraîche is similar to sour cream, but has a unique, slightly sour taste. If you're unable to locate crème fraîche at your supermarket, you can substitute sour cream. To make enough for this recipe, whisk ½ cup of chilled sour cream until it has doubled in volume and thickened slightly.

ACKNOWLEDGMENTS

The publisher would like to thank the companies and organizations listed below for the use of their recipes and photographs in this publication.

ACH Food Companies, Inc.

Cherry Marketing Institute

The Coca-Cola Company

Dole Food Company, Inc.

Kozy Shack Enterprises, Inc.

National Watermelon Promotion Board

Polaner®, A Division of B&G Foods, Inc.

The Quaker® Oatmeal Kitchens

Recipes courtesy of the Reynolds Kitchens

Unilever

PB Banana Muffins p. 27

Banana Freezer Pops, p. 77

METRIC CONVERSION CHART

VOLUME MEASUREMENTS (dry)

$\frac{1}{8}$ teaspoon = 0.5 mL
$\frac{1}{4}$ teaspoon = 1 mL
$\frac{1}{2}$ teaspoon = 2 mL
$\frac{3}{4}$ teaspoon = 4 mL
1 teaspoon = 5 mL
1 tablespoon = 15 mL
2 tablespoons = 30 mL
$\frac{1}{4}$ cup = 60 mL
$\frac{1}{3}$ cup = 75 mL
$\frac{1}{2}$ cup = 125 mL
$\frac{2}{3}$ cup = 150 mL
$\frac{3}{4}$ cup = 175 mL
1 cup = 250 mL
2 cups = 1 pint = 500 mL
3 cups = 750 mL
4 cups = 1 quart = 1 L

VOLUME MEASUREMENTS (fluid)

1 fluid ounce (2 tablespoons) = 30 mL
4 fluid ounces ($\frac{1}{2}$ cup) = 125 mL
8 fluid ounces (1 cup) = 250 mL
12 fluid ounces (1$\frac{1}{2}$ cups) = 375 mL
16 fluid ounces (2 cups) = 500 mL

WEIGHTS (mass)

$\frac{1}{2}$ ounce = 15 g
1 ounce = 30 g
3 ounces = 90 g
4 ounces = 120 g
8 ounces = 225 g
10 ounces = 285 g
12 ounces = 360 g
16 ounces = 1 pound = 450 g

DIMENSIONS

$\frac{1}{16}$ inch = 2 mm
$\frac{1}{8}$ inch = 3 mm
$\frac{1}{4}$ inch = 6 mm
$\frac{1}{2}$ inch = 1.5 cm
$\frac{3}{4}$ inch = 2 cm
1 inch = 2.5 cm

OVEN TEMPERATURES

250°F = 120°C
275°F = 140°C
300°F = 150°C
325°F = 160°C
350°F = 180°C
375°F = 190°C
400°F = 200°C
425°F = 220°C
450°F = 230°C

BAKING PAN SIZES

Utensil	Size in Inches/Quarts	Metric Volume	Size in Centimeters
Baking or	8×8×2	2 L	20×20×5
Cake Pan	9×9×2	2.5 L	23×23×5
(square or	12×8×2	3 L	30×20×5
rectangular)	13×9×2	3.5 L	33×23×5
Loaf Pan	8×4×3	1.5 L	20×10×7
	9×5×3	2 L	23×13×7
Round Layer	8×1½	1.2 L	20×4
Cake Pan	9×1½	1.5 L	23×4
Pie Plate	8×1¼	750 mL	20×3
	9×1¼	1 L	23×3
Baking Dish	1 quart	1 L	—
or Casserole	1½ quart	1.5 L	—
	2 quart	2 L	—